Published by Standard Publishing, Cincinnati, Ohio
www.standardpub.com

Printed in the United States of America

Acquisitions editor: Robert Irvin
Project editor: Kelli B. Trujillo
Cover and interior design: Jenette McEntire

Published in association with the literary agency of Credo Communications LLC, Grand
Rapids, MI 49525; www.credocommunications.net.

ISBN 978-0-7847-2230-5

15 14 13 12 11 10 09   9 8 7 6 5 4 3 2 1

dedication

This book is dedicated to ...

... our mothers, Mary Kay Meadows and Pat Cain, who first and best modeled for us that One Girl *Can* Change the World.

... our fathers, James Goad and Dayle Cain, who encouraged us to be Princesses with Purpose.

... and the student leaders of Hilltop Christian Camp Girls' Week, who are forever amazing us with your world-changing spirits.

get your shoes on!

Kim: Once my mom and I were sorting through the antique trunk where she stores keepsakes from my childhood. You know what I'm talking about. Every mom has a special place where she keeps your old report cards, baby clothes, trophies, the clipping from your first haircut—a time capsule for the milestones of your life. I was poring over some photos when she held something up and exclaimed, "Oh, look! Your first pair of shoes!" I glanced up in time to see her clutching them to her chest and then turning them around in her hands. "Look how tiny they are!" she said. "I remember when you took your first steps."

We bet your mom still has at least one pair of your baby shoes too. She may even have had them bronzed. Kim's granny prized her dad's so much that Kim inherited three pairs, right along with the family Bible.

What is it about a baby's first shoes? Could it be that a baby's first steps hold so much promise? Think about how much we praise a toddler when she takes her first awkward steps. We back up a few inches on our knees, hold out our arms, and coax, "Come on! You can do it!" Then, when she wobbles forward, we exclaim, "Look, everyone—she's walking!" It's as if we take those first steps and all around us begin to wonder, "Wow. If she can do *that,* I wonder what else she's capable of!"

In a similar way, God rejoices over *you* when you get your shoes on and take those first steps. In Acts 12:7, 8, we're told that Peter was in prison and bound with chains. "Suddenly an angel of the Lord appeared and a light shone in the cell. He struck Peter on the side and woke him up. 'Quick, get up!' he said, and the chains fell off Peter's wrists. Then the angel said to him, 'Put on your clothes and sandals.'" Claudia's dad used this story from Scripture to help her through a hard time. By asking her, "Do you have your shoes on?" Claudia's dad prompted her to do *her* part to prepare for the work God was about to do.

Kim: What is it about girls and shoes? Not long after we take our first steps, we develop an early infatuation—almost as if it's built into our DNA. When I was on a mission trip in Honduras, staying in an apartment above a medical clinic with twenty other people, the American missionaries and their daughter would often visit with us. Their toddler was obsessed with shoes (only she called them by their Spanish name, **zapatos**). Whenever she was in the apartment, the women in our group would mysteriously misplace their shoes. One day we finally caught the toddler in the act—she was stumbling from our bedroom into the common area wearing someone's high heels! Thereafter, whenever she'd visit, we'd exclaim, "Hide the zapatos!"

Whenever I see a little girl wearing a skirt and red cowgirl boots, I think to myself, "Now **there's** a girl who knows who she is and isn't afraid to be it!" At dress-up night at girls camp, my elementary-aged friend Rebecca dons a princess dress but keeps her green Crocs sandals on. She may be dressed head-to-ankles like a princess, but she knows there'll still be plenty of time to play in the creek before dinner. Our camp student leader friend Lauren wears a pair of purple and black high-top shoes that she designed herself on the Converse Web site. When our friend Sylva was preparing for a trip to France, the most stressful part of her packing was the shoes. She wanted to pack lightly but needed a different pair for every occasion. Why? Because shoes say something to the rest of the world about who we are. In the same way, God created you with passions and a personality that are uniquely suited to fulfill his purposes.

❧ Make This Yours!

So we hope you've got a copy of our book *One Girl Can Change the World* and you're ready to dive in and discover exactly how *you're* uniquely created and called to do just that. This journal is all about helping you get your shoes on—helping you really chew on and think through and pray about and figure out how the ideas we talk about in *One Girl Can Change the World* look in *your* life. So after you read each chapter in *One Girl*, flip open this book and read the stories we've got to share in the corresponding section of this journal. Then pause and reflect on the Stepping In, Stepping Up, and Stepping Out application questions and ideas.

Stepping In

The **Stepping In** questions with the flip-flop image are personal reflection questions designed to help you get your feet wet.

Stepping Up

The **Stepping Up** questions with the running shoe image are about stepping up your game and building discipline into your personal time.

Stepping Out

The **Stepping Out** questions with the high heel image are about using your own signature leadership style and giftedness to get out there and serve others.

You'll find lots of free space to write, scribble, and doodle your own thoughts, prayers, and questions. And if you flip toward the back, you'll see seven different sections for specific notes and ideas. We tell you all about them in chapter 2 of *One Girl Can Change the World*. So grab a pen and use this space to figure out just how God's called you to change your world!

Keep Moving

Kim: My mom tells me that I was walking at nine months, but I always had to be holding on to something until I was thirteen months old. I was too scared I'd fall. It didn't matter if it was the coffee table or someone's hand—as long as I was holding **something**. She said she'd hold out a ruler and coax me to grab on to the other end. She could trick me for a bit by letting go of her end of the ruler. For a while, I'd walk along unknowingly. But as soon as I realized that she no longer had the other end, I'd fall.

Don't be afraid. God rejoices over your first steps and eagerly anticipates where they will take you. Stay connected to him. Picture him on your level, a few inches ahead, coaxing, "Come on! . . . I've got you! . . . I won't let you fall!" I love these words from John Bunyan because they give a great image of taking those steps of faith.: "I have loved to hear my Lord spoken of; and wherever I have seen the print of his shoe in the earth, there have I coveted to set my foot too." [2]

After Hurricane Katrina, the Associated Press published a close-up photo of the feet of a young boy in New Orleans's Ninth Ward. In order to safely traverse the wreckage, he had made some crude shoes by attaching some cardboard packaging to the bottoms of his feet with rubber bands. In the picture the cardboard is turned upward at his toes so that you can see the writing on the product packaging. It says, "Keep Moving."

When you face obstacles, put your shoes on and *keep moving*. You were born to walk. You were born to be a world changer. Like Cinderella, if the shoe fits—wear it. And remember, like the little girl who stole our zapatos, there's always someone who looks up to you and is eager to try your shoes on. Someone is following you. Let this encourage you to take to heart Colossians 3:17: "Let every detail in your lives— words, actions, whatever—be done in the name of the Master, Jesus, thanking God the Father *every step of the way*" (*The Message*, italics added).

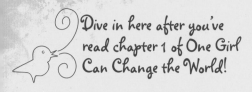

Dive in here after you've read chapter 1 of One Girl Can Change the World!

a princess with a purpose

> "No one but God can recognize you fully.
> No one but God can love you so completely.
> No one but God can fulfill your heart's deepest desires.
> No one but God can name you Princess."
> —Nicole Johnson [1]

Sarah Culberson, a seemingly average girl from Morgantown, West Virginia, had been adopted when she was one year old. She grew up in a very loving family, but, like many adopted kids, she couldn't help but wonder about her birth parents. Who were they? What were they like? Sarah finally overcame her fear of being rejected and, with the help of a detective, took what she calls one of the biggest risks of her life and tracked down her biological father. What she discovered was amazing. She found out that she is a princess . . . *literally!* Her father is Joseph Kposowa and her grandfather was Francis Kposowa, the Paramount Chief of the Mende tribe in Bumpe, Sierra Leone, Africa. Sarah discovered she's in line to possibly hold the title as Paramount Chief one day in a country she didn't grow up in.

When Sarah first visited Bumpe, she was indeed treated like royalty. She was presented with a traditional African dress, made of the same green print as the shirt her father wore. When they drove into the village, Sarah was greeted by a welcoming committee of hundreds of people singing and dancing while children ran alongside the car chanting her name. About a hundred men and women in the crowd were wearing clothing made from the same green print as her new dress. "I learned in the African tradition, when there is a special occasion everyone, men and women, in a family buy the same material and have outfits made," Sarah writes on her Web site (www.bumpenya.com). "They had already made me a part of the family and having a dress made that matched everyone else's made me feel that they were saying, 'you are one of us.' You have no idea how incredible it felt to be so honored and welcomed."[2]

In a special welcoming ceremony, Sarah was given a new Mende name: *Bumpenya,* which means "Lady of Bumpe." All of that could go to a girl's head, but Sarah is very humble about it. She said she thought to herself, *What did I do to deserve this?* and, *God, you have truly blessed me.* Part of Sarah's humility came from seeing firsthand the heartbreaking effects of the civil war that lasted over a decade and claimed an estimated sixty thousand lives and displaced over a million others. Her father is the headmaster of Bumpe High School, which had been ransacked by rebels. It was in desperate need of rebuilding.

In an interview on *Good Morning America,* Sarah said that when she saw the school's needs firsthand, she thought to herself, *I've come all this way for a reason. I've got to do something. I've got to help.*[3] After returning to the U.S., she started the Kposowa Foundation to raise the money that has paid for building construction, books, and furniture for the school. The foundation is now expanding its mission to help the community by providing wells for clean drinking water, student scholarships, transportation for students who have to walk as much as ten miles, and improved medical clinics. Though Sarah isn't interested in actually becoming Bumpe's Paramount Chief, she has answered a call. As she said in the ABC News interview, "The title princess means responsibility, and that's what I'm taking on."

So what about you? Do you believe that you are a princess with a purpose? Do you really believe 1 Peter 2:9—that you're part of "a chosen people, a royal priesthood, a holy nation, a people belonging to God, that you may declare the praises of him who called you out of darkness into his wonderful light"? Do you believe that you are "God's workmanship, created in Christ Jesus to do good works, which God prepared in advance" for you to do (Ephesians 2:10)?

Then what's stopping you from stepping out and achieving that purpose? What are you afraid of? For years Sarah Culberson was afraid that discovering the truth would mean rejection. Is that your fear too? Or could it be that you are afraid of change? Or of the unknown? Or is it possible that you fear you're not good enough? Spend some time thinking of what's keeping you from stepping out, and journal your thoughts in the space provided on these pages.

After taking what she describes as one of the biggest risks of her life in trying to find her birth father, Sarah Culberson was able to say to the *Los Angeles Times,* "I feel so blessed. I don't think it's any coincidence we were separated. I really think I was meant to help. That's why I was put on this Earth." [4]

Sarah got her shoes on, and God provided the miracle. As she sums up on her Web site, "This trip to Africa has changed my life and I have learned a great deal from my journey. The most important things I've learned are to be unstoppable, even in the face of fear, that the unknown doesn't have to be scary, to let go of the expected result, to always resolve unresolved relationships, and to take risks." [5]

Fashion designer Coco Chanel said that a woman should always leave the house dressed as if this is the day she has a date with destiny. Did you know that God has already clothed you for destiny? Galatians 3:27, 28 says, "For all of you who were baptized into Christ have clothed yourselves with Christ . . . you are all one in Christ Jesus." Isaiah wrote, "I delight greatly in the LORD; my soul rejoices in my God. For he has clothed me with garments of salvation and arrayed me in a robe of righteousness, as a bridegroom adorns his head like a priest, and as a bride adorns herself with her jewels" (Isaiah 61:10). And Colossians 3:12 says, "Therefore, as God's chosen people, holy and dearly loved, clothe yourselves with compassion, kindness, humility, gentleness and patience."

When Sarah was clothed with new garments that signified her place in the Bumpe community and was accepted as a princess—when she understood her destiny—she was moved by compassion and humility to make a difference. Our hope is that you also get that same strong sense of your identity as a princess with a purpose, and we hope the sense of who you're meant to be will move you to change the world.

Get Your Shoes On!

Stepping In

⚯ Read Psalm 139 twice—once silently and once out loud. How would this day be different if you really believed Psalm 139 was written to you?

⚯ Read 1 Peter 2:9, 10 from *The Message*: "But you are the ones chosen by God, chosen for the high calling of priestly work, chosen to be a holy people, God's instruments to do his work and speak out for him, to tell others of the night-and-day difference he made for you—from nothing to something, from rejected to accepted."

Our friend Sarah wrote this great poem. Check it out . . .

I Am a Princess

I'll never w a n d e r
    I'll never   stray
I'll walk with **You**
         Forever and a day.

My heart is **strong**
    So is my **will**
My heart is no **TOY**
    Nor Satan's to kill.

I am a *princess*
    The Lord is my King.
For with his power
    I can do anything.

Yes. I am a *princess*
    Righteous and true
For God made me beautiful,

        As he did *you*.

—© Sarah Arnold [6]

Now like our friend Sarah (who was fifteen when she wrote her awesome poem), try writing your own poem expressing what it means to you to be a princess with a purpose.

Stepping Up

⑥ Read these verses in your own Bible, then jot down your thoughts about what they've got to say to you:

🍃 John 1:12

🍃 John 15:15, 16

🍃 1 Corinthians 3:16

🍃 Colossians 3:12

◎ Sarah Culberson found out she was a princess—and it gave her a real sense of mission as she now works to help the people of Bumpe. How would *you* live differently if you began to think of yourself as a princess in disguise?

◎ Somewhere deep in your heart, you have a suspicion—a hope—that your life is meant to mean something. Dream a bit about something big you think might be in your future.

Stepping out

◎ Make a time line of your life, beginning with your birth and then listing the moments in your life up until now. Enter today's date on your time line. Now it's your turn. What will you do with your one and only life starting from this moment forward? Date and sign the line below when you're ready.

_____

Name   Date

"And who knows but that you have come to royal position for such a time as this?" (Esther 4:14).

"Let the Kingdom always be before you, and believe resolutely in things that are invisible."
—Evangelist, in John Bunyan's *The Pilgrim's Progress* [7]

"Whatever comes
. . . cannot alter
one thing. If I am a
princess in rags and
tatters, I can be a
princess inside.
It would be easy
to be a princess if
I were dressed in a
cloth of gold, but it is
a great deal more of
a triumph to be one
all the time when no
one knows it."
—Frances Hodgson,
A Little Princess [8]

"The King is enthralled
by your beauty; honor
him, for he is your lord"
(Psalm 45:11).

"I praise you because I am fearfully and wonderfully made; your works are wonderful, I know that full well" (Psalm 139:14).

"I want this to be imprinted in your minds: God still loves the world through you and through me *today*."
— Mother Teresa [9]

what's my passion?

> "If you give God the right to yourself,
> he will make a holy experiment out of you.
> God's experiments always succeed."
> —Oswald Chambers [1]

Claudia: I met with some amazing college students recently. As we were sitting around a table, eating bagels slathered with honey-flavored cream cheese, we talked about their passion to change the world. Zachary, a political science major, dreams of becoming president of the United States. Nathan wants to discover a cure for cancer. Bethany wants to be a missionary. Kristen wants to become a sports therapist. Though they have very different passions, they share a common desire to make a difference in this world for God. I told them how excited I was to hear their dreams, and then I shared my experience in the dolphin exhibit from chapter 2 of *One Girl*.

We will not just drift into our purpose. Like the girl with the handheld computer game at the dolphin pavilion, there are just too many distractions that threaten to keep us from God's best! As I write this it's not even yet lunchtime, and already there's unending noise in my world. It's hard to focus. I woke up to the disarming sound of the alarm clock. My cell phone is now ringing, my computer is buzzing, the coffeemaker is beeping, the TV is blaring . . . and I just got out of bed, for crying out loud! Not to mention the continual noise in my own head that can be just as annoying and even louder than the external noise. **Should I wash my hair? What will I wear? I feel fat! I need to whiten my teeth.** The internal noise that I generate all the time—my list of things to do and people to see—is never ending . . . and LOUD! If we don't get intentional about the big picture and discover our place on this planet, we'll get distracted by the bells and whistles and miss God's bigger blessings.

So this is your place to turn off all the noise and focus! Here it is: your chance to define your personal mission. Research shows that we are more likely to accomplish the goals that we write down, so get intentional about discovering God's best for you. As you turn back to these pages time and again to see what God has done, revel in the knowledge that he always accomplishes his purposes!

Get Your Shoes On!

Stepping In

⊚ Read Colossians 1:9-12 in your Bible. Then read it aloud using the words "I" or "me" like this:

God, I ask you to fill me with the knowledge of your will through all spiritual wisdom and understanding. And I pray this so that I can live a life worthy of you and can please you in every way: bearing fruit in every good work, growing in the knowledge of you, being strengthened with all power according to your glorious might so that I can have great endurance and patience, and joyfully give thanks to you, for you have qualified me to share in the inheritance of the saints in the kingdom of light.

⊚ Read Ephesians 2:10 in your Bible and then write the verse here. Next, circle the words in the verse that really stand out to you.

⊚ Devote time each day in prayer, asking God to reveal his desires for you. Tell him that you desperately want to fulfill his purposes for your life, and ask him to guide you in your search and to open the eyes of your heart so that you may see what he has in mind for you. Ask him to help you be obedient to him in following where he leads and to help you overcome any obstacles along the way.

Flip to the "What's God Saying to Me?" section at the end of this journal and take some time to write down what you think God may be saying to you during your prayer time, through his Word, or through other people and circumstances.

Stepping Up

⊚ Write out a prayer in your own words based on Ephesians 5:15-17.

⊚ Turn to the "My Life Mission" section at the back of this journal and answer the questions there. (Don't rush through it—take your time!)

Stepping out

◎ Write your personal mission statement in the "My Life Mission" section at the back of this journal. Remember, a personal mission statement should:

1. Be one sentence

2. Be easily understood

3. Make your heart beat fast when you say it

It should also include an action, a core value, and a target cause or group that you are most passionate about.

◎ Share your personal mission statement with at least one other person. Who will you share it with? Write that person's name here:

_____

Commit to checking in with each other from time to time to share what you're doing to fulfill your personal mission.

"This project has completely confiscated my life, darling. Consumed me as only hero work can."
—Edna, costume maker in The Incredibles [a]

"The place God calls you to is the place where your deep gladness and the world's deep hunger meet."
—Frederick Buechner [3]

"'For I know the plans I have for you,' declares the LORD, 'plans to prosper you and not to harm you, plans to give you hope and a future'" (Jeremiah 29:11).

"You have to start young
if you want to be a leader.
You can't just wait for it to
fall in your lap. You have
to take control."
—our friend Ellen Pashley

"Look at a day when you are
supremely satisfied at the end.
It's not a day when you lounge
around doing nothing;
it's when you've had everything
to do, and you've done it."
—Margaret Thatcher [4]

"A personal mission statement acts as both a harness and a sword— harnessing you to what is true about your life, and cutting away all that is false."
—Laurie Beth Jones, The Path [6]

"You have to find something that you love enough to be able to take risks, jump over the hurdles, and break through the brick walls that are always going to be placed in front of you."
—George Lucas [5]

Dive in here after you've read chapter 3 of One Girl Can Change the World!

what kind of leader am i?

> "Accept one another, then, just as Christ accepted you, in order to bring praise to God" (Romans 15:7).

So if you've just read chapter 3 in *One Girl,* you've spent some time thinking about what kind of Lollipop Leader you are. We're one big bag of assorted flavors . . . we're all different, and that's how God intended it to be. But have you ever noticed that we tend to get into groups with others who eat lollipops just the same way we do?

Claudia: I've heard it said that there are two types of people: those who take up space and those who "make space." A great leader is the kind of person who always "makes space." Drinking coffee at the local coffee shop the other day, I couldn't help but notice a group of girls talking and laughing in a tight circle. As I watched, a girl who I would say is so different she could create an individual lollipop category walked up and spoke to the group—and they all immediately tightened the circle as if to say "you don't belong" and continued to talk. But there was one girl in the group who **made space.** She moved over so the new arrival would have room, made eye contact, smiled, and patted the girl on the back as if to say, "There *is* room for you here." That girl—that making-space girl—is a true leader. A leader is someone who loves the people that God sent his Son to die for. In that brief moment I could tell that the making-space young woman is one girl who will change the world!

A friend of mine who played football for the Chicago Bears told me that the word **accept** that Paul uses in Romans 15:7 is like a picture of a player catching a football. He demonstrated how catching the football requires reaching out, grabbing hold, and then tucking it under to protect it. Wow. Isn't that what leadership is about? Reaching out, grabbing hold, and protecting what God has put in front of us? Leadership is about accepting and making space for all types of lollipop eaters—just as God made space for us.

❧Get Your Shoes On!

Stepping In ⟳

⊚ Grab a lollipop in your favorite flavor. Can you identify yourself from the Lollipop Leadership styles described in chapter 3? Are you a Chomper, Saver, Twirler, Strategist, Optimist, Critic, or Hider? Use this tool to help you figure out which leadership style best describes you . . .

Leadership Style Self-Assessment

1. Read through the following list and **cross out** seven of the descriptions that absolutely do **not** describe you.

Adventurous (C)

Assertive (F)

Camouflaged (B)

Cheerleader (D)

Conservative (E)

Creative (A)

Decisive (G)

Detail-Oriented (E)

Discerning (F)

Dreamer (A)

Goal-Oriented (G)

Idealist (D)

Insecure (B)

Logical (F)

Long-Term Visionary (E)

Motivator (A)

Nonconformist (A)

Opinionated (C)

Organized (G)

Overly Cautious (B)

Positive (D)

Problem Solver (G)

Questioning (F)

Resolute (C)

Resourceful (E)

Risk Taker (C)

Social (D)

Super Analytical (B)

2. Next, look at all the descriptions still in the list and circle the seven that **best** describe you. There will probably be more than just seven that fit you, but try to narrow in on those that match you perfectly!

3. To score yourself turn to the answer key on p. 37.

๏ Which Lollipop Leader type drives you crazy? Which kind of person is hardest for you to connect with? Why? Brainstorm some ideas here for ways you could better work with this type of person.

๏ Can you remember the first time you were given a lollipop? Read 1 John 3:1 aloud: "How great is the love the Father has lavished on us, that we should be called children of God! And that is what we are!"

How does eating a lollipop remind you that you are a child of God?

Stepping Up

◉ What happens to us as we grow up? We tend to get into our own group
of lollipop eaters and criticize those who do not eat lollipops the way we
do. One of the best ways a leader can step up is to accept the call from
God to love all his kids.

Read 1 John 4:19–21: "We love because he first loved us. If anyone
says, 'I love God,' yet hates his brother, he is a liar. For anyone who does
not love his brother, whom he has seen, cannot love God, whom he has
not seen. And he has given us this command: Whoever loves God must
also love his brother."

How can you step up in leadership? Who do you need to love who
you are now criticizing, avoiding, gossiping about, or getting annoyed by?

Stepping Out

◎ Read aloud 1 John 3:18: "Dear children, let us not love with words or tongue but with actions and in truth." Find a way to show love to one of God's children today. You might grab a bag of lollipops and share them with someone, such as a child, a classmate, a nursing home patient, a social outcast, or someone in youth group you don't know very well. Later write how you showed love right here:

Lollipop Leadership Style Self-Assessment Scoring

Beside each description on p. 33 is a letter. How many of each letter did you circle?

A= _____

B= _____

C= _____

D= _____

E= _____

F= _____

G= _____

Use this key to figure out which leadership type you most identified with.

If you circled mostly **A's**, then you might be a **Twirler.**

If you circled mostly **B's**, then you might be a **Hider.**

If you circled mostly **C's,** then you might be a **Chomper.**

If you circled mostly **D's,** then you might be an **Optimist.**

If you circled mostly **E's**, then you might be a **Saver.**

If you circled mostly **F's,** then you might be a **Critic.**

If you circled mostly **G's,** then you might be a **Strategist.**

"But of course we can't take any credit for our talents. It's how we use them that counts."
—Mrs. Whatsit in Madeleine L'Engle's *A Wrinkle in Time* [1]

"You have brains in your head. You have feet in your shoes. You can steer yourself any direction you choose."
—Dr. Seuss, from *Oh, the Places You'll Go!* [2]

"For we are God's
workmanship,
created in Christ
Jesus to do
good works,
which God
prepared in
advance for
us to do"
(Ephesians 2:10).

"Why are you trying so hard to fit in when you were born to stand out?"
—Ian in *What a Girl Wants* [a]

"Don't let anyone look down on you because you are young, but set an example for the believers in speech, in life, in love, in faith and in purity" (1 Timothy 4:12).

"Example is not the main thing in influencing others. It is the only thing."
—Albert Schweitzer [4]

"May he give you the desire of your heart and make all your plans succeed" (Psalm 20:4).

Dive in here after you've
read chapter 4 of One Girl
Can Change the World!

listen...

"All Scripture is God-breathed
and is useful for teaching, rebuking,
correcting and training in righteousness,
so that the man of God may be
thoroughly equipped for
every good work"
(2 Timothy 3:16, 17).

Kim: My dad and stepmother, Brenda, were celebrating my birthday with me, and I had just opened what I thought was the last of their gifts. Then I noticed that there was still a small box in the bottom of the gift bag. I winked at Brenda. "Is this one from you?" She nodded toward Dad and said, "Nope. Your dad picked that one out all on his own. He's had it for three months and couldn't decide whether to give it to you at Christmas or for your birthday." Dad hadn't picked a gift out without help for years, so I had a hunch something profound was coming.

I unwrapped the gift, and inside was a small pewter pendant that read, "I'm sending an angel ahead of you to guard you along the way" (a reference to Exodus 23:20, when God was leading the Israelites to the promised land). Dad had engraved on the back "To Kim, From Dad—2003." I was going through a personal struggle at the time, and my dad's sweet gesture caused me to sob . . . **really** sob. Then Dad got up from his chair and wrapped me in his arms while I cried. We didn't talk about it—I just cried while he held me.

I'll never forget that embrace because Dad died unexpectedly two weeks later. His death devastated me, and I still miss him terribly. But I know that I **know** that his gift on that birthday was a message from my Father—my heavenly Father—who knew what was yet to come and assured me that he would guard me along the way. Every time I hold that pendant, I take comfort in knowing that God is not surprised by the events in our lives. He knows our future because he's already there.

In chapter 4 of *One Girl Can Change the World,* we talk about how you can hear from God. God speaks to us through his Holy Spirit, through his Word, through his creation, through other people, and through experiences. In order to be a world changer, you must be deliberate about seeking God and hearing what he wants to speak into your life. And you do that by devoting time alone with him, reading his Word, and praying.

In his book *In a Pit With a Lion on a Snowy Day,* Mark Batterson says, "When we read Scripture, we are recruiting new nerve cells and rewiring neuronal connections. In a sense, we are downloading a new operating system that reconfigures the mind. We stop thinking human thoughts and start thinking God thoughts."[1] He goes on to describe a fascinating fact about our brains. It's something called the reticular activating system (RAS)—"a cluster of nerve cells" at the base of our brains. The way it works is this: as you go about your everyday life, countless images, sounds, and smells are flying at you. You couldn't possibly process all of those details or you wouldn't get much else done. The RAS creates "files" for all those things so that you can recall them when you need to at a later time. [2] For example, have you ever noticed how, when you buy a new purse, it seems like you start seeing that purse everywhere? Or when you're working on a paper for school on a topic you previously hadn't given much thought to, all of a sudden you start seeing details that relate to that topic? That's the reticular activating system. It's as if you've told your brain to think about something on the back burner, and it's now giving you the answers.

That's a great picture of how God speaks. When you spend time in prayer and reading his Word, your brain is creating file folders of information. Then, through his Spirit, God speaks to your heart by reminding you of the truths you've learned in your time with him. Jesus said in John 14:26 that the Spirit "will teach you all things and will remind you of everything I have said to you." When you get that nudging to call your grandmother or to tell a friend that you're sorry for the wrong you did or to turn from an area of disobedience or to take the next step in pursuing your purpose, more than likely that's God speaking to you.

We read in 1 Thessalonians 2:13: "And we also thank God continually because, when you received the word of God, which you heard from us, you accepted it not as the word of men, but as it actually is, the word of God, which is at work in you who believe." When you take in the Word of God, it goes to work in you. So take some time right now to be still, listen, and obey.

Get Your Shoes On!

Stepping In

◉ Take this journal outside. Are you there? Now read Romans 1:20: "For since the creation of the world God's invisible qualities—his eternal power and divine nature—have been clearly seen, being understood from what has been made, so that men are without excuse."

What does nature tell you about God? Sit still outside and talk to God. Use the space below (or the "What's God Saying to Me?" section at the back of this journal) to write down your thoughts about what God is saying to you through nature.

Stepping Up

◎ The primary way God talks to us is through his Word. Start today spending at least as much time reading the living, breathing Word of God as you do putting on your makeup or fixing your hair. And find a friend who can check in on you to see if you're keeping your commitment to read the Bible every day. Write your friend's name here:

_____

◎ Each day as you read the Bible, consider: Is God giving you any special insights as you read? If so, write it in the margin of your Bible and date it or write it in your journal. Is anything in the passage confusing? If so, write it down and pray about it. Make a point of asking your youth pastor or other godly person what they think it means.

◎ Use the "What's God Saying to Me?" section at the back of this journal to keep track of your thoughts as you continue to read God's Word. Also use that space to write down ways God may be speaking to you through conversations with others or through experiences.

Stepping out

6 Make a list of your family and friends. Next, spend some time praying for each of them. Then send them each a card or e-mail and tell them they were in your prayers today. Keep track of your specific prayers here, and jot down when God answers them.

"Your word is a lamp to my feet and a light for my path"
(Psalm 119:105).

"I have hidden your word in my heart that I might not sin against you" (Psalm 119:11).

"The heavens declare the
glory of God;
the skies proclaim the work of
his hands.
Day after day they pour forth
speech;
night after night they display
knowledge"
(Psalm 19:1, 2).

"As the deer pants for
streams of water,
so my soul pants for
you, O God.
My soul thirsts for
God, for the living
God.
When can I go and
meet with God?"
(Psalm 42:1, 2).

"The thing the devil
most fears is prayer!"
—Amy Carmichael [a]

"The God who created, names and numbers the stars in the heavens also numbers the hairs of my head . . . He pays attention to the very big things and to the very small ones. What matters to me matters to Him, and that changes my life."
—Elisabeth Elliot [4]

Dive in here after you've
read chapter 5 of One Girl
Can Change the World!

extreme makeover

> "Start by doing what is necessary;
> then do what is possible;
> and suddenly you are
> doing the impossible."
> —Francis of Assisi [1]

We're big fans of "dream boards." Perhaps you've created one for
your bedroom: a bulletin board with pictures cut out from magazines
that represent your hopes and dreams. We've already said that more
goals are accomplished when they're written down. In the same way
that our brains store those goals and work in the background to get
them accomplished, we believe there is great power in embedding images
in your mind of the goals you want to achieve. But the trouble with
dream boards (or any written or unspoken goal, for that matter) is that
they are worthless unless there is a *plan* to reach those dreams.

Kim: *Though storing the images in your brain may help
you to work on reaching them, they don't just fall in your
lap. You have to actually have a **plan** to get there. In high*

school, mine included a picture of the car I wanted to buy when I turned sixteen (a red convertible VW bug), a picture of the boy I wanted to date, a picture of an athlete with the toned body I wanted to achieve, and a picture of the college I wanted to attend. But I couldn't get the car without first considering how I'd in fact **pay** for it, and I couldn't pay for it until I actually got a job and saved my money. I would never be able to date the curly-haired, dreamy leading man in the school dramas without spending countless hours learning his schedule and figuring out how to bump into him at his locker and preplanning what I would actually **say** to him once I did. I'd never get the athlete's body without some pain and sweat. (This one I never did achieve.) And I'd never get into the college I desired without focusing on my GPA and studying for the SATs.

In chapter 5 of *One Girl*, we talk about the importance of developing a plan to support your goals. God's will includes a plan, and that plan includes you. So doesn't it stand to reason that you should be intentional about discovering your part in his plan?

What if your passion is to create fabulous handbags that will one day be sold the world over? How do you change the world by creating handbags, you ask? Here's how: One day when you become a wildly successful Kate Spade, you commit to donating a portion of your profits to a cause that God has placed on your heart. You treat your employees and suppliers well. And when the Council of Fashion Designers of America awards you "America's New Fashion Talent in Accessories," you give God the glory and use your platform to honor him. But in order to get to that platform, you must first have a plan. You'll have to devote many hours researching what women want in handbags and illustrating your ideas. You may need to get into a fashion design school. You may, like Kate Spade, decide to land a job in the accessories department at *Mademoiselle* magazine.

Sara Blakely created Spanx®, the brand of footless pantyhose and other body shaping garments, with just five thousand dollars. Not initially knowing anything about the industry, she started by reading books on patents at the library after work, researching branding and packaging and beating the streets to talk to any manufacturer who would listen to her dream. Once she had a prototype, she landed an appointment with a buyer from Neiman Marcus and actually dragged the buyer to the ladies room where she showed her the before-and-after results of wearing Spanx. Then she coerced all her friends to go to Neiman's (and eventually Saks Fifth Avenue, Nordstrom, and Bloomingdale's) to make a big to-do over the product. [2]

Today Spanx has a massive retail sales presence, and Sara has created the The Sara Blakely Foundation, "dedicated to helping women globally and locally through education and entrepreneurship." She recently donated a million dollars to The Oprah Winfrey Leadership Academy for Girls—South Africa. Sara says she's out to change the world, one body at a time. [3]

The point is, you will actually need to *get your shoes on* and put feet to your mission. Why not start by using this journal as a sort of dream board that relates to your mission, passions, and what you've heard God saying to you about how you will change the world? On the following pages, write your mission statement in big bold letters. Next, spend some time writing the steps it will take for you to get there. Remember, there are three things a good plan should do:

1. Start with the end in mind.

2. Be specific.

3. Include deadlines.

Grab a stack of magazines and cut out pictures that represent your mission. Then *do the thing*—work your plan!

❧Get Your Shoes On!

Stepping In ⟋

⊚ We don't know what the "bugs" are in your life, but you do. You know what particular sins, habits, and bad attitudes infest your life and keep you from being a clean dwelling place for God's Spirit. Find some time alone with God. Cry out with David as you read Psalm 51:10-13: "Create in me a pure heart, O God, and renew a steadfast spirit within me. Do not cast me from your presence or take your Holy Spirit from me. Restore to me the joy of your salvation and grant me a willing spirit, to sustain me." If you want, write out your prayer here:

⑥ Take some time right now to write down some specific "bugs" God has brought to mind. If you want to get creative, doodle actual *bugs* on this page and label them. Then draw a big *X* over each bug, representing your belief in God's forgiveness and restoration.

Stepping Up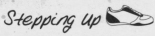

⊚ Create a dream board by cutting out pictures from magazines that represent your goals. Place it where you will see it every day, or keep the pictures in the pocket at the back of this journal.

Stepping Out

⊚ How can you honor God with the day ahead? Make a plan. List specific ways, right here, that you will honor God for the next twenty-four hours.

⑥ Now think about how you'll take some time over the next week to bless someone who's close to you, like a parent, a sibling, a close friend, or a mentor. Plan something specific you'll do to really encourage and love on that person. Jot your notes here:

"He who wants milk
should not sit on a stool
in the middle of the pasture
expecting the cow
to back up to him."
—Unknown

"Chance favors the
prepared mind."
—Louis Pasteur [4]

"The LORD Almighty
has sworn, 'Surely, as
I have planned,
so it will be, and
as I have purposed,
so it will stand'"
(Isaiah 14:24).

"But the plans of the LORD stand firm forever,
the purposes of his heart through all generations"
(Psalm 33:11).

"Many, O LORD my God, are the wonders you have done.
The things you planned for us no one can recount to you;
were I to speak and tell of them, they would be too many to declare" (Psalm 40:5).

"In him we were also chosen, having been predestined according to the plan of him who works out everything in conformity with the purpose of his will" (Ephesians 1:11).

"Consecrate yourselves, for tomorrow the LORD will do amazing things among you" (Joshua 3:5).

"Therefore, since we are surrounded by such a great cloud of witnesses, let us throw off everything that hinders and the sin that so easily entangles, and let us run with perseverance the race marked out for us" (Hebrews 12:1).

Dive in here after you've
read chapter 6 of One Girl
Can Change the World!

passing the punch-bowl test

> "They may forget what you said,
> but they will never forget
> how you made them feel."
> —Carl W. Buechner [1]

No doubt you're familiar with the popular reality show *The Bachelor*. The premise is this: if you take twenty-five beautiful, single young women yearning for love, cram them together in a house for about six months where their every move is recorded, make them compete through individual and group dates for the attention of one good-looking, successful guy, and then eliminate the women one-by-one in a rose ceremony at the end of each episode, the result will be everlasting, true love between the guy and one lucky woman.

And the bachelor will go to great lengths to find that one true love. In season 5, bachelor Jesse had his best friend Jenny pose as one of the bachelorettes and act as a spy. Byron of season 6 eventually chose Mary, who was later arrested for punching him in the face. In season 11, Brad broke hearts by becoming the first bachelor in the show's history unwilling to choose either of the two finalists. In season 13, Jason proposed to Melissa in the finale, but then broke off the engagement with her on the follow-up show and asked out the other finalist instead. Of the first thirteen seasons, only one couple remains together at the time of this writing. Seems true love is a bit harder to find than the producers think!

Matchmaking is serious business. Just ask Abraham's chief servant. He was sort of a biblical-times Chris Harrison (*The Bachelor* host). In Genesis 24, Isaac is single, handsome, and incredibly wealthy—a perfect candidate for *The Bachelor*. His father, Abraham, is aging and concerned about the available Canaanite bachelorettes, so he asks his chief servant to play matchmaker: "I want you to swear by the LORD, the God of heaven and the God of earth, that you will not get a wife for my son from the daughters of the Canaanites, among whom I am living, but will go to my country and my own relatives and get a wife for my son Isaac" (vv. 3, 4). So the chief servant heads out of Dodge and, to sweeten the pot, we're told that he takes ten camels and "all kinds of good things" (v. 10). (Don't you wonder what those "all kinds of good things" were? No doubt they included jewelry and chocolate!)

So the matchmaker approaches the town of Nahor and stops at the well outside the town when evening is approaching and the women will be coming to draw water. (Smart thinking. Going door-to-door would have been much less efficient!) But now what? How does he decide which girl is right for Isaac?

The Bachelor's application for hopeful bachelorettes simply asks for a photo, age, height, weight, and occupation. But the eligibility requirements are much more extensive. Among the list of twenty-three requirements, couched in language that requires a law degree to read, is this one:

> All applicants must authorize Producer to conduct
> a background check, which may include, without
> limitation, a credit check, a military records check,
> a criminal arrest and/or conviction check, a civil
> litigation check, a family court litigation check,
> interviews with employers, neighbors, teachers, etc.
> All applicants must sign the attached Authorization
> to Release Personal and Confidential Records and
> Information.

Whoa! And this one:

> Bachelorette(s) must agree to live, participate and
> cooperate with the other individuals and the Producer
> during the taping of the Program . . . Bachelorette(s)
> must be able to travel for long periods of time, must be
> adaptable to various living situations, and must enjoy
> participating and living in close proximity with others
> of varied background and experience.

OK, sort of like band camp. But what about this one?

> All applicants understand and acknowledge that
> participation . . . may expose applicant . . . to the
> risk of death, serious injury, illness or disease and/or
> property damage. Applicants must be willing and able

to participate in physical activities such as: skydiving, snow skiing, ice skating, parasailing, water skiing, rollerblading, and the like. Applicants must sign a release attesting to the fact that the applicant understands and knowingly and willingly agrees to assume such risks. [2]

Background checks and "ability to get along with others in tight living quarters" seem like a small price to pay for finding true love . . . but "risk of death, serious injury, illness or disease"?! Honey, no man is worth that! Luckily our matchmaker/chief servant in Genesis 24 has only one eligibility requirement, and it's very simple: "Bachelorette must, after having been asked for a drink of water, offer to water my camels too."

Seriously, that's what he says. Well, OK, it was more like this: "Then he prayed, 'O LORD, God of my master Abraham, give me success today, and show kindness to my master Abraham. See, I am standing beside this spring, and the daughters of the townspeople are coming out to draw water. May it be that when I say to a girl, 'Please let down your jar that I may have a drink,' and she says, 'Drink, and I'll water your camels too'— let her be the one you have chosen for your servant Isaac. By this I will know that you have shown kindness to my master'" (Genesis 24:12-14).

You see, our matchmaker was looking for what we call an "and-then-some" kind of girl. A girl who would go the extra mile. A girl like Sylva who once surprised Kim by shoveling the snow off her driveway. *And then* left a box of hot cocoa and a Valentine's Day card on the porch. *And then* fashioned a heart out of sticks in the snow. A girl like the barista at the Starbucks coffeehouse who prepared Claudia's foam latte *and then* drizzled chocolate syrup in the shape of a smiley face on top of the whipped cream. A girl like Kim's great-aunt Bea who, when Kim's single mother was raising three children and had frozen pipes one winter, came while everyone was out of the house and loaded up two sinks' worth of dirty dishes. Bea took the dishes to her house, washed them, brought them back, put them away, *and then* left a pot of chili on the stove. A girl like the senior citizen at church who could say she's given a lifetime of service and is ready to rest but instead serves in the nursery *and then* cooks meals for shut-ins. A girl like the student leader who works her heart out all week at camp *and then* stays in touch with campers all year long. *These* are "and-then-some" kind of girls.

Abraham's matchmaker/chief servant was praying for an "and–then–some" girl for Isaac. And God answered his prayer immediately. The text says, "Before he had finished praying, Rebekah came out with a jar on her shoulder" (Genesis 24:15). After she went to the spring and filled her jar, our matchmaker hurried up to meet her and said, "Please give me a little water from your jar" (v. 17). And we're told that she quickly gave him a drink *and then* said, "I'll draw water for your camels too, until they have finished drinking" (v. 19). Now a thirsty camel can drink up to ten gallons of water. Our matchmaker had ten camels. Ten gallons, ten camels. It's possible that Rebekah ran back and forth to the well, carrying a total of a hundred gallons of water! Now *that's* an "and-then-some" kind of girl!

While she was doing all this running and filling and watering, verse 21 says "the man watched her closely to learn whether or not the LORD had made his journey successful." (You'd think he'd have had a pretty good idea after the first fifty gallons, but whatever. Some matchmakers are cautious.) When the camels had had their fill, our matchmaker "took out a gold nose ring . . . and two gold bracelets." (Ah, told you there must have been jewelry!) Then he asked whose daughter she was and if there was room at her father's house for him and the camels to spend the night. And she said, "We have plenty of straw and fodder, as well as room for you to spend the night" (vv. 22-25).

Then our matchmaker put the ring in her nose and the bracelets on her arms and then he fell to the ground and said, "Praise God! I've found an and-then-some girl for Isaac!" (or something like that). Then Rebekah's family sent her off with our matchmaker. And just as Isaac was going out to the field one evening to meditate (no doubt on why it was taking the matchmaker so long), he looked up and saw all the camels approaching. At the same time Rebekah looked up and saw Isaac. He saw her, she saw him, the matchmaker introduced them, and Isaac said, "Rebekah, will you accept this rose?" (or something like that). The last verse of the chapter says, "So she became his wife, and he loved her" (v. 67). Better odds than *The Bachelor*!

The point of this story is not to get you to water camels so you'll find the perfect husband! In *One Girl,* we talk about the importance of having good character, no matter what your specific leadership style. Along with honesty, courage, humility, and vision, character includes being willing to serve. It's about saying, "I'll not only do this, but I'll do this for you as well." When your mom asks you to clean your room, you clean up the kitchen too. When your kid sister needs help with her homework, you offer to help the next night too. When the game is over, you help your coach pick up the equipment. When the new kid at school asks for directions to class, you offer to walk her there.

How do you change the world? You start by loving the person in front of you . . . *and then some.*

Get Your Shoes On!

Stepping In

⊚ Who are some of your heroes? Who are the women in your life or from history who inspire you? Look at this list of traits and write the name of at least one woman you know personally or you've heard about beside each trait. (You can write the same person more than once!)

Character

Servant Attitude

Courage

Humility

Willingness to Be Led

Ability to Inspire Vision

⊚ Now, on a scale of 1 to 5 (1 being "needs much improvement" and 5 being "I'm better at this than anyone I know"), rate *yourself* as a leader in each of the following areas:

Character

Servant Attitude

Courage

Humility

Willingness to Be Led

Ability to Inspire Vision

⊚ Now circle one of the items on the list that you *most* want to focus on developing in your life. Why?

Stepping Up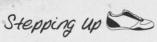

◎ What's one thing you need to do today that would take courage? Do it!

◎ Do one act of service in secret today—one you won't get any recognition for. After you do it, write what it was here:

◎ Today strive to ask at least three people, "How can I help you?" Then, at the end of the day, come back here and write some quick notes about who you helped and how you helped them.

Stepping Out

◉ Brainstorm a list of things you could do *now* to serve others (ideas: visit an elderly neighbor, volunteer to teach English to immigrants through your local library or a local chapter of World Relief [www.worldrelief.org], clean out your closet and have a garage sale to donate money to charity, start a prayer group, send a letter of encouragement to someone, help deliver meals through Meals on Wheels [www.mowaa.org], and so on).

◎ Make a list of the character traits you want to be known for. Then find a teacher, friend, or mentor to share your vision with. Tell them, "These are the specific character traits I'm working on." Ask them to hold you accountable when they see you behaving contrary to those traits. List some specifics here:

"The smallest good act today is the capture of a strategic point from which, a few months later, you may be able to go on to victories you never dreamed of."
—C. S. Lewis [3]

"I don't know what your destiny will be, but one thing I do know: the only ones among you who will be truly happy will be those who have sought and found how to serve."
—Albert Schweitzer [4]

"Now that I, your Lord and Teacher, have washed your feet, you also should wash one another's feet. I have set you an example that you should do as I have done for you" (John 13:14, 15).

"Lootie had very foolish notions concerning the dignity of a princess, not understanding that the truest princess is just the one who loves all her brothers and sisters best, and who is most able to do them good by being humble towards them."
—George MacDonald, The Princess and the Goblin [8]

"Do nothing out of selfish ambition or vain conceit, but in humility consider others better than yourselves" (Philippians 2:3).

"But the fruit of the Spirit is love, joy, peace, patience, kindness, goodness, faithfulness, gentleness and self-control. Against such things there is no law" (Galatians 5:22, 23).

Dive in here after you've read chapter 7 of *One Girl Can Change the World!*

burpees are better together

> "He who walks with the wise grows wise,
> but a companion of fools suffers harm"
> (Proverbs 13:20).

As we told you in chapter 7 of *One Girl,* we've started a new workout routine that includes these killer calisthenics called "burpees." Burpees are a tortuous form of exercise that just about kill us every time! But we've discovered an amazing principle: burpees are better together. The only way either of us are able to get out of bed and to the gym by 6:30 AM three days a week just to face the torture is because we know the other will be there right alongside us, encouraging us and reminding us of the end goal.

We are best as a team. Jesus started team building by investing in twelve leaders who changed the world. People are so into the team thing that we bet if we could peek into your closet, we'd find at least one shirt that supports your favorite team. Think about it—our culture *loves* teams! Take fantasy football, for example. Fantasy football offers a way to "buy" your own professional franchise and become coach, owner, and president of a team. The Fantasy Football Care Web site offers to focus on fantasy football 365 days a year. If you are "one girl" who has read the book and now are working in this journal, you will need to learn to lead a team!

Perhaps someone has noticed your leadership ability and has asked you to lead in some area. Think about something you have been asked to do, like make treats for the club you have joined, provide childcare for a women's Bible study, or help raise money for a mission trip. How can you invest in the people around you? By *using* people to get the job done? No way! Use the *job* to get the people done! We recommend that you look around and invite people to join you to get the job done who are passionate, have good character, and are willing to hold you accountable as you strive to succeed.

Has no one invited you to lead yet? Then look around and offer to help someone! Eleanor Roosevelt, a former first lady, said, "I could not, at any age, be content to take my place in a corner by the fireside and simply look on." [1] In her lifetime, she led teams in the areas of women's rights, the League of Women Voters, the Navy-Marine Corps Relief Society, and the Red Cross.

Our friend Shelly was taking a child development class when she noticed moms in her church who looked like they could use a break. She invited some of her friends to help her facilitate a mom's day out on a

Saturday close to Christmas so they could shop child-free. The event was such a success that the church continues to offer it year after year. Shelly is certainly one girl who is changing the world . . . and her original team of five has grown to over fifty!

How about you? What needs do you see around you that ignite your passions and could use your leadership? Take a cue from world changers like Eleanor Roosevelt and Shelly and know that you will achieve more goals faster and better by inviting others to join you. Burpees are better together.

Get Your Shoes On!

Stepping In

◎ What parts of your efforts so far to fulfill your life mission have been like burpees to you—really tough, tiring, and maybe even torturous?

⊚ Who in your life has led you to know God better? List three people who have encouraged you to know God and grow in your love for him. Pray for them.

Stepping Up

⑥ Who exhibits the character traits you want to model? Could one of those people become your coach? Andy Stanley says a coach does three things: observes, instructs, and inspires. And remember, start by asking for her help one step at a time: observing you in action or giving you feedback on some ideas. Over time, the more she's given you constructive input and the more she gets involved in your efforts, she will naturally have become your coach . . . without the word ever having come up. Jot down some notes here about who might make a good coach in your life:

Stepping out 👠

⑥ Who might compliment your strengths and weaknesses in helping you to meet your goals? Invite a team to help you take a stand for something or someone. How about developing a team to make treats for teachers, give the bus driver donuts, or help assist with special needs students? Write down some notes here (or in the "My Team" section at the back of this journal) about who's already on board with your mission and names of people you want to draft to your team.

"What I can do, you cannot.
What you can do, I cannot.
But together we can do
something beautiful for
God."
—Mother Teresa [2]

"Two are better than one,
because they have
a good return
for their work"
(Ecclesiastes 4:9).

"As iron sharpens iron,
so one man
sharpens another"
(Proverbs 27:17).

"Let the wise listen and add to their learning, and let the discerning get guidance" (Proverbs 1:5).

"Plans fail for lack of counsel, but with many advisers they succeed" (Proverbs 15:22).

"Listen to advice
and accept
instruction, and
in the end you
will be wise"
(Proverbs 19:20).

Dive in here after you've
read chapter 8 of One Girl
Can Change the World!

catfighters and backbiters

> "The crisis of today
> is the joke of tomorrow."
> —H. G. Wells [1]

Kim: I'll never forget my most humiliating catfight. I was in junior high, riding the bus to school one sleepy Monday and oblivious to what was about to happen. As soon as I got off the bus, Amy was waiting for me at the flagpole. Amy was, let's say, a little rough around the edges—someone I steered clear of. She immediately got in my face, pushed me, and started ranting about how I'd better stay away from her boyfriend. It took me a second to comprehend who her boyfriend was, but I soon connected the dots and figured out he was a guy who'd been in my neighborhood over the weekend. (Apparently the guy had made a big deal of our playing flag football together, no doubt to make her jealous on purpose.) It was one of my most embarrassing moments. A crowd quickly gathered and watched as I tried to explain that I had no interest in her boyfriend (in part because I had no respect for his football skills). Luckily for me, the morning bell rang and the immediate crisis was averted. But I was never able to make amends with Amy, and we were enemies throughout school.

Since then I've learned something about how to resolve conflict. My skills were tested as an adult, when an incident happened that was just as silly as the misunderstanding with Amy. I was on my way to work one day when I received a call from my friend and human resources manager that we needed to talk as soon as I got into the office. It seemed that another girl in the office was in a tizzy, saying that some others had overheard me calling her "fat" at a company-wide meeting the day before.

"**What?!**" I shrieked into my cell phone. First of all, she **wasn't** fat (she was pregnant, but I would **never** call a pregnant woman fat; I think pregnancy is an all-around beautiful thing). Secondly, I've never made fun of anyone's physical appearance in my life, especially with regards to weight. (I am a fierce opponent to anything that would contribute to poor self-image because I've got several friends who've struggled with eating disorders.) Where on earth did she get **that?**

My friend said, "I don't know. I couldn't believe it myself. I asked her, 'Kim **Goad** said that?!' She says two or three other girls approached her after the meeting and told her that they'd overheard your comments, and she's very hurt." Luckily I'd had some lessons in dealing with conflict since the Amy incident and assured my friend that of course I didn't say these things and that I would deal with it head-on.

By the time I arrived at work, the office was all abuzz with the drama. My boss was meeting with the offended girl's boss. The human resources manager was meeting with her boss. Women were whispering about it in the bathroom. Absolutely no actual work was getting done. I went straight to the offended girl and, as the gossip girls were looking on, took her to a private office to talk. I told her that I didn't know what she heard but assured her that I said no such thing, had not even discussed her name, and that I think pregnancy is one of God's greatest miracles. I could tell she didn't believe me (she was still too hurt), but I'd said all I could say and we shook hands and agreed to try to move on. Next, one by one, I pulled aside her coworkers. Without accusing anyone, I explained that this gossip was going around and that I wasn't sure what had been heard, but that I absolutely had not said what they thought they had heard. Then I pulled my boss and her boss into an office and explained the same, told them what I'd done to correct the situation, and urged them to stop wasting so many man-hours on this issue and to press forward.

As I sat with them I said, "I've been replaying yesterday's meeting over and over in my head and can't, for the life of me, figure out what might have been misconstrued." Then the light bulb went on. In the meeting the day before, the human resources manager told me that she had bought Ben & Jerry's ice cream for the employees to enjoy at the end of the meeting. Noting my favorite flavor, I replied, "Ooh! Did you get Chubby Hubby?" As it turns out, the offended girl's last name rhymes with "hubby." The eavesdroppers thought I had called her "chubby"! We had wasted the entire morning in closed-door meetings trying to resolve how fudge-covered, peanut-butter pretzel ice cream had been twisted into an untruth!

What about you? Have you ever been falsely accused? Or have you said or done things that caused conflict? Whether it was accidental or purposeful, know this: to be a world changer, you've got to master the fine art of quashing the catfights. Pray. Go. Just between the two of you. Get over your silly self. H. G. Wells said, "The crisis of today is the joke of tomorrow." We like to put it this way: the hurts of today are tomorrow's ice cream treats.

Get Your Shoes On!

Stepping In

⦿ Make your own list of some of the mean things girls do to each other. Include mean behaviors you've been the victim of *and* mean behaviors you've done to others.

⊚ Read aloud James 4:1, 2: "What causes fights and quarrels among you? Don't they come from your desires that battle within you? You want something but don't get it. You kill and covet, but you cannot have what you want. You quarrel and fight."

This verse reminds us of the seagulls in the movie *Finding Nemo*. They fly around, squawking "Mine, mine, mine!" all the time. What is it that we, as girls, want more of? What is it that causes us to be a "mean girl"? Write some thoughts below and then talk to God about the desires that battle within.

Stepping Up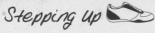

⊚ Read John 21:20, 21: "Peter turned and saw that the disciple whom Jesus loved was following them. . . . When Peter saw him, he asked, 'Lord, what about him?' Jesus answered, 'If I want him to remain alive until I return, *what is that to you?*'" (italics added).

Who are you looking around at and, just like Peter, asking, "What about her, Lord? She is so smart, pretty, tall, talented, skinny, popular . . . What about her, Lord?" Pause and hear Jesus say, "Get over your silly self."

Stepping out

◎ Who have you been mean to? Who has experienced your mean girl self?
Come on. Her name comes right to your mind. The girl you have hurt by
shunning, gossiping about, or just plain old mean girl stuff. Picture her.
Pray for her. Reach out to her and make it right.

If you want, write your prayer here:

"God blesses those who work for peace, for they will be called the children of God" (Matthew 5:9, NLT).

"If your brother sins against you, go and show him his fault, just between the two of you. If he listens to you, you have won your brother over" (Matthew 18:15).

"Do not let the sun
go down while
you are still angry,
and do not give
the devil a foothold"
(Ephesians 4:26, 27).

"Therefore, as God's chosen
people, holy and dearly
loved, clothe yourselves with
compassion, kindness, humility,
gentleness and patience. Bear
with each other and forgive
whatever grievances you may
have against one another.
Forgive as the Lord forgave
you. And over all these virtues
put on love, which binds them
all together in perfect unity"
(Colossians 3:12-14).

"Remember that everyone you meet is afraid of something, loves something, and has lost something."
—H. Jackson Brown Jr. [a]

"Do you remember
in kindergarten, how you'd meet
a kid, and know nothing about
them, then ten seconds later you'd
be playing like you were
best friends, because you didn't
have to be anyone
but yourself?"
—Gabriella in
High School Musical [a]

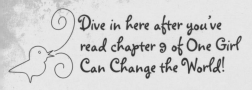
just keep swimming

> "Whatever you do,
> work at it with all your heart,
> as working for the Lord,
> not for men"
> (Colossians 3:23).

One thing that helps us is what we like to call the "Whatever Principle." You're no doubt familiar with the way people sarcastically say, "Whatever!"—you roll your eyes, shrug your shoulder, and lean your head when you say it. You may even make a big *W* with your fingers. But the apostle Paul gives the word *whatever* a new meaning for us. He says, *"Whatever* you do, work at it with all your heart, as working for the Lord, not for men" (Colossians 3:23, italics added). This statement is part of a letter Paul wrote from a prison in Rome to remind us that, in every activity, we can choose to honor God.

We don't know what problems you'll face on the way to your

goals—you may be facing huge obstacles even right now in this moment. Sometimes life is just really hard . . . sometimes the distance between who you are and who you want to be seems insurmountable. But remember that Paul wrote those words from *prison,* so he knew what it meant to face hardships.

Your goal may seem far off, but there's always a *next thing* you can do. When facing a problem, this "Whatever Principle" can help you honor God by doing the next right thing that's in front of you. If we get this principle and do our best to apply it, we can overcome any problem. You can always do the next right thing, no matter what life throws at you.

Claudia: Kim and I are always getting lost. We were working out in the gym at church just yesterday and went the wrong direction when we left the gym. (Yeah, we're talking about the gym we go to several times a week!) Recently I drove along with my friend Alan to a lunch meeting. Because of my poor sense of direction, you can imagine how blown away I was when his car ~~spoke~~ to him! In a very confident voice, his car said, "Turn right at the next four-way stop." Oh, my goodness! Alan just tells the car his destination and it guides him there.

For less than one hundred dollars anybody can buy a gadget that will fit in your pocket and tell you exactly where you are on the earth. The Global Positioning System (GPS) is a constellation of twenty-four Earth-orbiting satellites developed by the U. S. Department of Defense. Each of these solar-powered satellites circling the globe weighs two thousand pounds. A GPS receiver locates the satellite, figures out the distance, and uses the information to find its location. [1]

All this is based on a simple math principle called trilateration (which, thankfully, you don't have to understand in order to use GPS!). In fact, simplified versions of this invention are now available to anyone who is tired of being lost. They now make personal navigation devices so user-friendly, you can use them right out of the box! Claudia's husband just purchased a GPS unit for fishing. By simply typing in the *waypoint* (GPS language meaning "location"), this handy device will record the spot where you last caught fish so you can find it again. Amazing!

The "Whatever Principle" Paul wrote about can help us find our way through any obstacle. We can use his teaching as our own personal GPS system as we navigate through problems. Although this letter was not written directly to us, it was written *for* us to help us set our waypoints, which will guide us to a life of joy through living an extreme Christian life. Paul makes the destination very clear in Philippians 3:8: "I consider everything a loss compared to the surpassing greatness of knowing Christ Jesus my Lord." And in verses 12-14: "Not that I have already obtained all this, or have already been made perfect, but I press on to take hold of that for which Christ Jesus took hold of me. Brothers, I do not consider myself yet to have taken hold of it. But one thing I do: Forgetting what is behind and straining toward what is ahead, I press on toward the goal."

Claudia: I think Kim is a master at practicing the "Whatever Principle." As we were writing **One Girl,** Kim was caring for her mother who was dying of pancreatic cancer. Kim felt lost and confused, uncertain about the future. Have you ever been there? Have circumstances ever made you feel like you've lost your way? As I watched Kim face one of the biggest obstacles of her life, she practiced the "Whatever Principle"—she lived her moments by doing the next right thing. She told me that before she got out of bed in the morning, not sure what the day would hold, the next right thing for her was to pray these simple words: "Help . . . Help . . . Help! Thank you . . . Thank you . . . Thank you." For Kim, the "Whatever Principle" meant daily acknowledging her need for God and her gratitude to him.

We don't know where you are in your journey today. Maybe you're facing your parents' divorce. Maybe you've given in to an unhealthy habit and can't see your way out. Maybe you've done something that has threatened your reputation. Maybe a relationship has been severely damaged or seemingly severed for good. Maybe you're a senior in high school and have no idea what you want to do with your one and only life. But this we do know: the next right thing is always available. Repeat Kim's prayer—"Help . . . Help . . . Help! Thank you . . . Thank you . . . Thank you."—and find someone to talk to. Can't you just hear Paul whispering, "Press on toward the goal. You can do it. Whatever!"?

Get Your Shoes On!

Stepping In

⊚ Read James 1:2-4. Has this Scripture proven true in your own life? If so, how?

⊚ When Paul was in a Roman prison, he was able to say that his obstacles had actually served as a testimony to draw others to Christ. When David was called to slay Goliath, he said, "The LORD who delivered me from the paw of the lion and the paw of the bear will deliver me from the hand of this Philistine" (1 Samuel 17:37). Can you think of a time when God used *your* obstacles as opportunities? Recall God's faithfulness to you by making a list of your own "The-Lord-who-delivered-me-from . . ." situations from your past.

⊚ When you've finished with your list, look up Romans 8:31 in your Bible and read it. Then write what this verse means to you here:

Stepping Up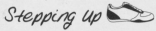

⑥ What is it that you are afraid of? If you don't face your fears, you're going to miss out on some great adventures! Make a list of three things you are afraid of.

⑥ Read aloud Isaiah 41:10 and then talk to God about the fears you've just written down.

◎ Does perfectionism keep you from moving forward? What are some details you need to let go of so you can just do whatever it is you feel called to do?

Stepping out

⑥ Reach out to someone who is facing an obstacle today and pray for that person. Look around. There are obstacles everywhere and girlfriends who need encouragement.

"You were running a good race. Who cut in on you and kept you from obeying the truth? That kind of persuasion does not come from the one who calls you" (Galatians 5:7, 8).

"Consider it pure joy, my brothers, whenever you face trials of many kinds, because you know that the testing of your faith develops perseverance. Perseverance must finish its work so that you may be mature and complete, not lacking anything" (James 1:2-4).

"Never allow a person to tell you no who doesn't have the power to say yes."
—Eleanor Roosevelt [2]

"The one who is in you is greater than the one who is in the world" (1 John 4:4).

"Life is an endless struggle
full of frustration
and challenges,
but eventually
you will find a hair stylist
you like."
—Unknown

"We are always on the anvil; by trials God is shaping us for higher things."
—Henry Ward Beecher [a]

"Obstacles are those frightful things you see when you take your eyes off your goal."
—Henry Ford [5]

"When things are horrible—just horrible—I think as hard as ever I can of being a princess. I say to myself, 'I am a princess . . .' You don't know how it makes you forget."
— Frances Hodgson Burnett, A Little Princess [6]

"No mistake was made in heaven when God gave you a gift of leadership or teaching."
—Nancy Beach [7]

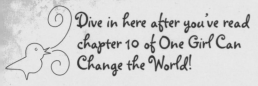
blowing it big time

> "How gracious he will be when you cry for help! As soon as he hears, he will answer you" (Isaiah 30:19).

Claudia: In chapter 10 of **One Girl,** I tell a story about a little boy named Jason and the hammer he threw. God used that little boy to show me that God looks at our hearts, not our hammers. One time, after sharing the Jason story with a small group of teenage girls, I asked them, "Where do you see yourself in this story? Are you the criminal, the wounded child, or the teacher?" Jessica was first to answer: "It depends on the moment and the time of the month!" The group laughed. But then everyone quickly became serious and shared a moment when they remembered holding a hammer and feeling like a criminal. I then shared with the group a "hammer moment" so terrible we could hardly wrap our minds around it. Tragedy hit the family of Christian musician Steven Curtis Chapman when their seventeen-year-old son accidentally ran over and killed their five-year-old daughter Maria Sue Chapman. Can you even **imagine** the feelings they're dealing with? The famous songwriter and singer said, "Every lyric I've ever written has been tested beyond what I ever imagined." Will, his seventeen-year-old, said, "Faith is the only way I can tell myself she's okay. She's safe in the arms of Jesus." [1]

If you've experienced failure, wounded someone you love, or just plain blown it big time, take a moment and put yourself in this scenario. There's an angry circle of important leaders surrounding a woman who has been caught in the sin of adultery. Have you ever read this story in John 8:1-11 and pictured yourself as the woman? Can you imagine yourself, like the woman, caught—caught in the sin of lies or gossip or some other area of disobedience and had your sins publicly exposed? Jesus steps into the circle and, as always, brings grace. He writes some words in the dirt and, one by one, everyone leaves. When only Jesus and the woman remain there, he stands up, looks at her, and asks the same question he asks you and me—the same question he asks for anyone who has ever failed.

Imagine Jesus looking into your eyes and asking you this question:

"'Woman, where are they? Has no one condemned you?'

'No one, sir,' she said.

'Then neither do I condemn you,' Jesus declared. 'Go now and leave your life of sin'" (vv. 10, 11).

Can you relate to this woman who looked into the face of Jesus and received forgiveness? Can you picture Jesus saying, "I don't condemn you"?

Claudia: At Maria Sue Chapman's memorial service, Will's brother Caleb spoke. He said, "We prayed for a healing for Maria, but he healed her in a way that we all didn't like. But he's gonna heal my brother in a way that I think we're all going to like a lot." [2] His statement drew applause and cheers from the crowd because we all can relate to the need to be healed from our hammer moments. I picture Will, Jason, the woman caught in adultery, you, and me running to Jesus with our hammers, falling into his loving arms, and accepting amazing grace. The God who made you and knows you—the one who created everything you can see and all that you can't—sees your heart, not your hammer. God is not a police officer in Heaven waiting to thump you on the head, but rather a loving Father waiting with his arms stretched to give you boundless love and eternal forgiveness.

Get Your Shoes On!

Stepping In

◎ Where do you see yourself in the Jason story? Are you the wounded child, the teacher, or one of the kids observing the crime from the playground? Take some time writing why.

◎ How do you picture God? Do you see him as a police officer in Heaven waiting to catch you doing something wrong? Or is God the teacher who sees your heart and not your hammers?

◎ Read Romans 8:28 and then spend some time in prayer, giving God your hammers. Rest in the truth that he sees your heart.

Stepping Up

◎ Get quiet. Breathe deeply. Ask God to let you know from the tip of your head down through your neck, shoulders, fingertips, and legs and then to the tip of your toes that he loves you. Right now, this very minute, let his love surround you.

Stepping out

◎ Think about a time when a friend had blown it big time with you. Did you see her heart or her hammer? How could you have handled the situation differently? What do you need to do now to make it right?

◎ How can you show unconditional love to others in your life today?

"He does not treat us as our sins deserve
or repay us according to our iniquities.
For as high as the heavens are above the earth,
so great is his love for those who fear him;
as far as the east is from the west,
so far has he removed our transgressions from us"
(Psalm 103:10-12).

"I never look back, darling!
It distracts from the now."
—Edna, in
The Incredibles [3]

"See if there is any
offensive way in me,
and lead me in the
way everlasting"
(Psalm 139:24).

"If a true princess has
done wrong, she is always
uneasy until she has
had an opportunity of
throwing the wrongness
away from her by saying:
'I did it; and I wish I had
not; and I am sorry for
having done it.'"
—George MacDonald,
The Princess and the
Goblin [4]

"Humble yourselves
before the Lord, and
he will lift you up"
(James 4:10).

"What lies behind us and
what lies before us are tiny
matters compared to what lies
within us."
—Ralph Waldo Emerson [5]

"Your past does not equal
your future."
—Unknown

"My brokenness
is a better bridge for
people than my pretend
wholeness ever was."
—Sheila Walsh [6]

remember

After the Israelites miraculously crossed the Jordan River, God told Joshua to choose one man from each of the twelve tribes to pick a stone out of the place where the priests had stood in the river. The stones must have been large, because the men were commanded to carry them on their shoulders. Joshua positioned them on the other side of the Jordan where the people were camping that night and explained:

"In the future, when your children ask you, 'What do these stones mean?' tell them that the flow of the Jordan was cut off before the ark of the covenant of the LORD. When it crossed the Jordan, the waters of the Jordan were cut off. These stones are to be a memorial to the people of Israel forever" (Joshua 4:6, 7).

God's people created a memorial because it is *so* important for us to pause and remember what God has done in our lives! When we forget how faithful he's been to us, we can lose our way and cower in the face of obstacles. But when we remember how he has come through in the past, it helps us face our current fears. The Bible emphasizes over and over and over again how important it is to truly *remember* God's work and his faithfulness in our lives. For example . . .

- ☉ "Remember the wonders he has done, his miracles, and the judgments he pronounced" (1 Chronicles 16:12).
- ☉ "I will remember the deeds of the LORD; yes, I will remember your miracles of long ago" (Psalm 77:11).
- ☉ "I remember the days of long ago; I meditate on all your works and

consider what your hands have done" (Psalm 143:5).

◎ "Remember the former things, those of long ago; I am God, and there is no other; I am God, and there is none like me" (Isaiah 46:9).

During her freshman and sophomore years, Laura experienced depression and loneliness. At youth group she'd lean against a wall away from the others, silently praying that God would help her overcome her shyness and loneliness. One night she was leaning in her usual place and tears slid down her cheeks. She prayed, "Please get me out of this endless hole! I want to live again!", but says she felt like her prayers bounced off the ceiling. Then one night her youth pastor asked how she was doing. When she finally admitted her feelings of loneliness and despair, he spoke these words to her: "Laura, you need to walk on the water in faith. You've memorized verses since you were a little girl; now you're gonna have to put them to work."

What he was essentially telling her was, *Remember.* Laura decided to put his words to the test and memorized Philippians 4:13: "I can do everything through him who gives me strength." She walked into youth group the next week with these words in her mind and on her heart and found that she had the courage to initiate a conversation with another girl. It was the beginning of what she calls her "Life Extreme Makeover."

Over the next few months, she began to see real change in her life and within herself. She says she started stepping out more and making new friends. She says, most importantly, she learned that she is not alone. Now she notices other girls who are standing on the sidelines and comes alongside them in their loneliness to draw them out. She says, "The makeover experience was incredible, but I know that Jesus' power alone gave me the courage to face my fears of rejection and talking. He gave me the words to speak when I couldn't think of anything to say. It only took one encounter with the power of God to change my life forever." [1]

Laura knew the Bible and she knew the truth, but she just needed to really *remember*. She needed to take time to reflect on all God had already done in her life—and that gave her the courage to face the future with strength and confidence.

So how about you? You've read *One Girl Can Change the World*. You've gotten through this journal. What do you want to stop, right now, and remember? How has God been working in your life through your own "One Girl" experience? How has he spoken to you? How has God been faithful to you? How have you experienced his love or his guidance? What obstacles has God helped you deal with? What steps have you taken with God's help?

Rather than concluding the journal with *our* words, we want you to wrap up with *yours*. Fill the next few pages with your own "memorial"— words that honor God for the specific things he's done in your life during your journey through this book.

God, I want to always remember how you . . .

my life mission

◎ Three things that give me energy are:

◎ What did I always want to be when I grew up?

◎ If I won the lottery, what would I do with the money?

◎ What does a great day look like for me?

◎ What causes do I really care about most?

◎ What certain people groups (ex: kids, elderly, special needs, poor, other nationalities) do I really care about most?

☺ Here is everything I've accomplished so far. What am I really good at?

☺ Who do I admire the most? Why?

◎ These are books I like to read:

◎ What do I want to be most remembered for?

◎ What does my perfect life look like?

◎ What would I attempt if I could not fail?

⑥ How do I think God may be using all this toward my life mission?

⑥ Write your life mission. Remember, it should:

1. Be one sentence

2. Be easily understood

3. Make your heart beat fast when you say it

It should also include an action, a core value, and a target cause or group that you are most passionate about.

My mission is to _____

for _____ .

my plan

"If people can't see what God is doing, they stumble all over themselves; but when they attend to what he reveals, they are most blessed" (Proverbs 29:18, The Message).

"How precious to me are your thoughts, O God! How vast is the sum of them!" (Psalm 139:17).

"Speak, for your servant is listening"
(1 Samuel 3:10).

what's God saying to me?

"Delight yourself in the Lord and
he will give you
the desires of your heart"
(Psalm 37:4).

"Whether you turn to the right or to the left, your ears will hear a voice behind you, saying, 'This is the way; walk in it'" (Isaiah 30:21).

"Life is choices: always choose to do what you will remember ten years from now."
—Richard A. Moran [1]

✳ "But the Counselor, the Holy Spirit, whom the Father will send in my name, will teach you all things and will remind you of everything I have said to you" (John 14:26).

my team

"Only those who will risk going too far
can possibly find out how far one can go."
—T. S. Eliot [2]

"Luck? I don't know anything about luck. I've never banked on it . . . Luck to me is something else: hard work—and realizing what is opportunity and what isn't."
—Lucille Ball [a]

"All the days ordained
for me were written
in your book
before one of them
came to be"
(Psalm 139:16).

my progress

"So do not fear, for I am with you;
do not be dismayed, for I am your God.
I will strengthen you and help you;
I will uphold you with my righteous right hand"
(Isaiah 41:10).

"You gain strength, courage, and confidence by every experience in which you really stop to look fear in the face....You must do the thing you think you cannot do."
—Eleanor Roosevelt [4]

resources

"I remember the days of long ago; I meditate on all your works and consider what your hands have done" (Psalm 143:5).

"Search me, O God, and know my heart;
test me and know my anxious thoughts"
(Psalm 139:23).

"Perseverance is failing
nineteen times and
succeeding the twentieth."
—Julie Andrews [5]

ideas

"Life can only be understood backwards;
but it must be lived forwards."
—Soren Kierkegaard [a]

"He who began a good work in you will carry it on
to completion until the day of Christ Jesus"
(Philippians 1:6).

endnotes

Introduction—Get Your Shoes On!

1. Bette Midler, "Exclusive: Bette Midler Interviews the Divine Miss M," *After Dark,* May 1978, http://www.betteontheboards.com/boards/magazine-19.htm (accessed March 5, 2009).

2. John Bunyan, "The Eighth Stage," *The Pilgrim's Progress*, http://www.classicallibrary.org/bunyan/pilgrim/22.htm (accessed March 17, 2009).

1—A Princess with a Purpose

1. Nicole Johnson, *Keeping a Princess Heart: In a Not-So-Fairy-Tale World—A Conversation Guide for Women* (Nashville: W Publishing Group, 2004), 138.

2. Sarah Culberson, "Sarah's Story," http://www.bumpenya.com (accessed March 13, 2009).

3. Sarah Culberson, interview by Robin Roberts, *Good Morning America,* ABC, September 19, 2006.

4. Kelly-Anne Suarez, "Princess Finds the Shoe Fits," *Los Angeles Times,* September 15, 2006, http://articles.latimes.com/2006/sep/15/local/me-princess15 (accessed March 17, 2009).

5. Sarah Culberson, "Sarah's Story," http://www.bumpenya.com (accessed March 13, 2009).

6. Copyright © Sarah Arnold, used with permission.

7. John Bunyan, *The Pilgrim's Progress in Modern English,* L. Edward Hazelbaker, trans. (Gainesville: Bridge-Logos Publishers, 1998), 112.

8. Frances Hodgson Burnett, *A Little Princess* (New York: Penguin Books, 2002), 105-106.

9. Mother Teresa of Calcutta, "Charity: The Soul of Missionary Activity,"

accessed online at http://www.adelaide.catholic.org.au/sites/
CatholicMission/media/files/1162.doc (March 17, 2009).

2—What's My Passion?

1. Mark Pritchard, "The Experiment of Faith," *Monday Ministry Minutes*, http://
   www.facultyinc.com (accessed March 17, 2009).

2. Dialogue from "Movie Quotes from *The Incredibles*," http://homevideo.
   about.com/library/weekly/aa_movie_quotes_the_incredibles_a.htm
   (accessed February 20, 2009).

3. Mark R. Schwehn and Dorothy C. Bass, eds. *Leading Lives that Matter*
   (Grand Rapids: William B. Eerdmans Publishing Company, 2006), 112.

4. Margaret Thatcher, http://thinkexist.com.

5. George Lucas, http://thinkexist.com.

6. Laurie Beth Jones, *The Path* (New York: Hyperion, 1996), xvii.

3—What Kind of Leader Am I?

1. Madeleine L'Engle, *A Wrinkle in Time* (New York: Dell Publishing, 1962), 84.

2. Dr. Seuss, http://thinkexist.com.

3. Dialogue from "Memorable Quotes for *What a Girl Wants*," *Internet Movie
   Database*, http://www.imdb.com (accessed January 8, 2009).

4. Albert Schweitzer, http://www.brainyquote.com.

4—Listen . . .

1. Mark Batterson, *In a Pit with a Lion on a Snowy Day* (Colorado Springs:
   Multnomah Books, 2006), 46.

2. Ibid., 134-135.

3. Sam Wellman, *Amy Carmichael: For the Children of India* (Uhrichsville:
   Barbour Publishing, 1998), 183.

4. Elisabeth Elliott, "CQ Daily Archives: February 2000," *The Timothy Report*, http://www.timothyreport.com/february2000.html (access February 3, 2009).

5—Extreme Makeover

1. Francis of Assisi, http://www.brainyquote.com.

2. Information in this section was taken from "Sara's Story" on The Official Site of Spanx, http://www.spanx.com (accessed March 18, 2009).

3. Information in this section was taken from http://www.sarablakelyfoundation.com.

4. Louis Pasteur, http://thinkexist.com.

6—Passing the Punch-Bowl Test

1. Carl W. Buechner, http://thinkexist.com.

2. "The Bachelor: Eligibility Requirements" *The Bachelor* Web site, http://thebachelor.warnerbros.com/bachelor/eligibility.html (accessed March 18, 2009).

3. C. S. Lewis, *Mere Christianity* (New York: Simon & Schuster Inc., 1980), 117. *Mere Christianity* by C.S. Lewis copyright © C.S. Lewis Pte. Ltd. 1942, 1943, 1944, 1952. Extract reprinted with permission.

4. Albert Schweitzer, http://www.brainyquote.com.

5. George MacDonald, *The Princess and the Goblin* (New York: Puffin Books, 1996), 199.

7—Burpees are Better Together

1. Eleanor Roosevelt, http://thinkexist.com.

2. Mother Teresa, "Mother Teresa's Message to the UN's Fourth World Conference on Women," open letter written September 1995, http://www.ewtn.com/New_library/MT_woman.htm (accessed March 8, 2009).